UNDERSTANDING THE BODY OF CHRIST

Its Purpose, Our Need; And Why Church Still Matters Today

Brian E. Crouch

Contents

Chapter 1 - Modern Thought Opposes the Church

WE LIVE IN AN AGE of spiritual decline. It seems like people, in general, are becoming increasingly influenced by living in an immoral society and the mindset that comes along with it. Every day we are inundated with messages, values, and ideals that are in opposition to God, His church, and His purposes.

I am reminded of what Jesus said in Matthew 16:18 b, "I will build My church, and the gates of hell shall not prevail against it." Jesus has, in fact, established His church on this earth with Himself as the Cornerstone. The church has spread, grown, and developed for centuries upon centuries. That much is true. Nevertheless, though the gates of hell shall not prevail against it, we do know the devil relentlessly attempts to stall, diminish, and destroy God's covenant body of people through false teachings, inner division, physical attack, political opposition, and one of his most effective tactics: spiritual slumber.

As a nation, zeal for God is squelched under a persistent liberal agenda that exalts mankind and "self" while increasing attempts are made to sweep God and any mention of Him, under the table. Furthermore, we are asked and expected to be compliant, tolerant, and even participate in the silencing of morality and divine advocacy in this country. As a result, there is a noticeable generational decline among our young people today concerning their interest and attendance in church. This appears to reverberate upwards into older age groups who are likewise affected by cultural influences and the church's softening whisper. Perhaps now more than ever we need a second Reformation to purge the church of falsity while contemporaneously crying out to God for true revival to spread across this land. We have remained silent far too long.

What hurts us today is that we live in an age of individualistic expression, reliance, and inflated importance. For years now the message emitting from society is that life and happiness are all about us. Moreover, truth is whatever you want it to be or what seems best to you, your goals, and your desires. This changes constantly and from person to person since moral absolutes have been eliminated and "truth" is now relative to each individual. Unfortunately, even Christians fall into the ditch of these worldly ideas and principles. After years of exposure and hype, it's possible to be influenced and then convinced that we are at liberty to dictate which Scripture does or does not apply to us and view its commands and application as relatively optional. Or, even to avoid such things altogether and then pioneer something that suits us, personally or that puts our preferences centerstage. Perhaps maybe you have bought into the idea that a Christian does not actually need the Church and instead, you can now replace the formal assembly of God's people with an informal discussion of God at Starbucks or a park, or wherever. Some say if "we are the Church" then the Church is wherever we happen to be at the time and is not confined to traditional and historic assemblies within a "building". As a result, some have decided to alter biblical essentials for the sake of personal convenience. Thus, the church as we know it gets categorized as something outdated and unnecessary. This diminishes both the status and influence once exerted by the church. I attribute this largely to theological liberalism that pushes a view that conforms itself to trends and culture and whatever these exalt or deem important. In a determined effort to blend in with the environment, liberal Christianity does so at the expense of both truth and tradition. Their ideas are predicated upon a worldly view and philosophical way of thinking. To be clear concerning two forms of liberalism: *theological liberalism* eats at the church from the inside whereas *secular liberalism* does so from the outside. These two systems of thought are compatible. Both suspiciously question traditional views regarding divine authority and seek to replace it with human logic and reasoning. Both uphold science as the ultimate factor of determining truth. Each desires a sense of worldly status and recognition with disregard to the integrity and inerrancy of God's Word; and the help of historic confessions and creeds of the church. Additionally, "outside" secular liberalism shapes and forms the thinking of the "inside" liberal Christian. In this way, the ideas and philosophy of one permeate the other. Historically and presently speaking, this has never benefited the church in positive ways. Thus, this book contends for the orthodox conservative approach to the meaning, value, and significance of God's church. For now, and in light of our present discussion; ultimately both forms of liberalism are founded upon what is known as humanism and secularism.

The effects of humanism and secular ideology have permeated our school system, public arena, marketing, and value system.[1] These are not new problems, but rather have been around in some form for centuries.

Humanism finds its roots in ancient Greece, pre-Socrates. The concept revolves itself around the premise that "man is the measure of all things"[2]and that human beings alone are the "ultimate being and the ultimate authority."[3] This idea has trickled its way down through the centuries where it picked up

---

[1] For further information on these topics the author recommends Dr. R. C. Sproul's book describing the landscape of opposing world views in this country that are prevalent today and in opposition to Biblical thought, structure, and values. . . . . . It is titled, "Making a Difference", published by Baker.

[2] Making a Difference (Impacting Culture and Society As a Christian) by Dr. R. C. Sproul (Baker 1986); pg 60

[3] Making a Difference; pg. 60

both speed and traction during the 18th Century and the period of the Enlightenment when humanism became a dominating force in culture. It still is today.

Humanistic philosophy is what is known as *anthropocentric.* This is a compound word that is easily understood when it is broken down into two parts. The first part is "*Anthropos.*" This comes from the Greek language and means "*man.*" The second part of the word is "*centric*" which is where we get the word "*center.*" Thus, the word anthropocentric means something that is centered on man, i.e.: man-centered.

In contrast, the conservative approach is that we, as believers, have built our lives upon what is known as "*theocentric,*" or God-centered. We believe that God is the measure of all things and that He is the absolute being and the ultimate authority to behold; not man.

Whether we realize it or not, every day we are immersed in cultural values and ideas that stem from humanistic roots. This proverbial weed has grown like a kudzu vine that has strangled and overtaken our Christian morals and beliefs. This is precisely why when our children enter the arena of public schools and colleges, they are systematically torn from their Christian upbringing and the foundation that we have lovingly worked to build their faith, morals, values, and lives upon. Yet, our society that screams for tolerance is unable to tolerate any view that centers itself on the divine. Our culture is repulsed by the idea that we aren't on the throne, hold the keys, or get to determine what's right and wrong. In response, our children's growth as believers gets challenged, attacked, and choked out by humanistic philosophy.

Maybe you have seen the movie "God's Not Dead" where all of this is accurately played out. In the movie, a young Christian college student is pressured to abandon his faith, discard his values, and conform to the idea that God does not exist, that He is in fact dead, and if anything He is a fallacy created by a weak religious mindset. This movie accurately portrays what we are talking about here. As Dr. R. C. Sproul has observed, "Religion, in the modern humanistic view, tends to keep people in a conservative frame of mind, holding onto outdated and antiquated values." [4] In other words, the humanist believes that as the ultimate measure of all things, they are intrinsically capable of ridding the world of pain and suffering with enough time, effort, science, industry, technology, and education. Therefore, theocentric beliefs are neither welcomed nor tolerated by a militant humanist. Moreover, the battleground for their ideology is fought, daily, in the classroom. The problem is, there is no known resistance here and so they have already won by default. This is not to say that there aren't any Christian teachers in the public school system. Logically speaking, believers permeate many areas of our society. But what I'm bringing attention to here is the fact that as a nation,

---

[4]   Making a Difference; pg. 68

what is being taught in our schools is anything but Christian. Consequently, "our children are being taught one set of values in the home and the church, while they get another philosophical system through public education."[5]

As it occurred in the movie, the teacher relentlessly insisted and threatened that God was a religious concoction made up to pacify people and that true greatness and true freedom can only be achieved when we shake off this religious concept and instead trust in ourselves and our own abilities to make society and this world better. That's the difference between humanism and Christianity; anthropocentric and theocentric. The ultimate question is who is at the center of existence and importance: man or God.

As stated, the problem for us today is that our public school curriculum is decided and formulated by secular people who have a secular mindset and belief system. This word "*secular*" has its origins in Latin and is defined as meaning "*world*." Thus, something that is secular refers to this world in the here and now. In addition, anything concerning the eternal is outright denied or at the very least, is considered to be utterly skeptical. A secularist's viewpoint suggests that either the eternal doesn't exist, or even if it does, it is beyond our reach to understand it. So the idea is conveniently swept away. You can't have two centers. You either trust in God or you trust in yourself. For

---

[5] Making a Difference; pg. 71

the secularist, their focus remains on self, this world, and the here and now. It should be no surprise, then, that secularism and humanism are close friends. They share a disdain for God and the eternal and a love for self and the temporal. Unfortunately for us, this is the primary system of thought that is actively shaping the values and minds of our children. And we pay them thousand and thousands of dollars in tuition every year to do this.

It isn't just the schools that exert influence on the value system in this country. Hollywood is also a major contributor to the voracious appetite for promoting a humanistic worldly agenda in America.

An overwhelming majority of celebrities do not embrace the Christian faith. Many who do profess some sort of religion claim Buddhism, Hinduism, New Age, or Scientology. Yet others are outspoken atheists, agnostics; or vaguely consider themselves to be "spiritual" minded and void of any specific designation. Others have instead embraced the humanist philosophy we have adequately described. *None* of this shares commonality with biblical Christianity.

Unfortunately, Hollywood's presiding influence on our culture and society is unprecedented. Their human-centered worldly thinking assimilates itself through the release of movies, music, opinions, trends, and lifestyles they model and promote. Our children are surrounded by the idea that this life and this world are all that matters. Do what you want. Be who or what you want. It is this predominant philosophy that lies under the surface of the increasing levels of pride, narcissism, perversion, sexual immorality, and abortion – all of which eat at this country like cancer. When God is removed from our schools and the public arena, and when Christian values fade into the background until they disappear; the only thing left is *rot*.

As our country increasingly embraces a liberal, worldly mindset, our moral and value system degrades into a further downward spiral. God is misrepresented, generalized, watered-down, spiritualized, or left out altogether. What remains is human thought and decisions void of God's direction, authority, and counsel. We see this clearly today with the continuation of abortion and the exaltation of homosexuality. Interestingly, this latter agenda grew its strength and recognition from riding in on the coattails of a legitimate issue. Essentially what happened is during the movement for racial equality the LGBT community progressively asserted that a person's *sexual preference* is likewise a Constitutional "right." They recognized the softening of tense relations in this country as people began working together to resolve issues of racism and inequality. Seizing the opportunity, the homosexual agenda has been marketed and promoted to sell their idea that gay marriage, cross-dressing, transgender operations, gender dysphoria, and godless sexual immorality are also inherent "rights" that are worthy of Constitutional protection, allowance, and equality. This campaign has been followed by consistent and progressive marketing to desensitize our mindset to embrace these ideas. Consider the increase just over the last ten years of books, commercials, and movies that have actively portrayed and promoted the homosexual lifestyle.

Few primetime shows are void of at least one homosexual sex scene. Public schools now teach sexual gender as being optional. The Biblical definition of marriage is being challenged, ridiculed, and threatened to be replaced. People wearing woman's dresses and makeup yet having male anatomy are demanding the 'right' to use bathrooms specifically designed, labeled, and secured for females. Meanwhile, cross-dressers and transgenders are promoting reading books and storytelling to our small children in our public libraries. As a nation, we're being told to kindly accept, tolerate, make room for, and even embrace such craziness.

My point is *not* that one sin is or isn't worse than another, or that any person, idea, or lifestyle can't be powerfully transformed by God's saving grace; but rather, as a country we are steadily headed toward increased moral upheaval and depravity that is squarely centered on relative truth and liberal, humanistic thought. And that to some degree; self-exaltation, self-reliance, and God minimizing liberal principles have entered into the Church thereby influencing how we view His commands, holiness, authority, and importance in our lives. For thousands of years now, the devil has consistently promoted his agenda that we are better off on our own. This idea gains its desired traction when the people of God begin to adopt a secular mindset. Evidence of this appears when we begin to shun corporate fellowship and worship and replace it with whatever suits us.

In contrast, the church is needed for the continued growth and nourishment of God's people and for renewing our minds theocentrically (Ephesians 4:19-24, Romans 12:1-2). Instead of conforming ourselves to the standards of this fallen world we live in, we are to be transformed by a progressive Spirit-led change in our thought and behavior that comes through God's Word, obedience to His instruction, and time spent worshipping in His presence.

Over time, God's Holy Spirit will increasingly emit through us as we live among our secular neighbors, co-workers, and fellow citizens. One day, this might be used by God to lead some to saving faith in Jesus Christ. As we learn to view both sin and mercy as God does, we will likewise conform to Paul's timeless instruction to Timothy; "the Lord's servant must not be quarrelsome but kind to everyone, able to teach, patiently enduring evil, correcting his opponents with gentleness. God may perhaps grant them repentance leading to a knowledge of the truth, and they may come to their senses and escape from the snare of the devil, after being captured by him to do his will" (2 Timothy 2:24-25). Because ultimately, that is precisely the problem we see in this world today: Fallen human beings raising their voices and fists at God in rebellion to His presence, Holiness, and that which He desires of us – to know Him, love Him, obey and worship Him in spirit and truth (John 4:24, 17:3). And guess what? At one point, we were rebels of truth, too.

Interestingly, according to Paul's letter to Titus, before salvation, we were no better than they are. He writes, "For we ourselves were once foolish, disobedient, led astray, slaves to various passions and pleasures, passing our days in malice and envy, hated by others and hating one another" (Titus 3:3). This is further confirmed in the book of Ephesians where Paul says; 'And you were dead in your trespasses and sins in which you once walked, following the course of this world, following the prince of the power of the air, the spirit that is now at work in the sons of disobedience among whom we all once lived in the passions of our flesh, carrying out the desires of the body and the mind, and were by nature children of wrath, like the rest of mankind" (Ephesians 2:1-3).

That's our past resume before salvation. At this point some might say to me; "those verses of Scripture are describing someone else. I have never wrestled with such passion or immorality before or after salvation." Comparably, that may be true. Perhaps Satan has never tempted you in these areas and those sins have never manifested into the many spiritual strongholds that might result. Yet Paul leaves no one out. For in the very least we were all "foolish, disobedient, and led astray .... and were *by nature* children of wrath, like the rest of mankind." Everyone has been affected.

Sin is all-inclusive. Even the most civilly virtuous (yet unsaved) among us are impure, unrighteous, and have fallen short of the glory of God (Isaiah 64:6, Romans 3:23). Sin has corrupted human nature even in our birth and this alone would keep anyone from entering heaven (Psalm 51:5, Isaiah 59:1-2).

Prior to the finished work of Christ being applied to our souls, we were all descendants of Adam's seed. This seed represents sin and death that has been spread to all mankind as a result of the Fall. Just as death often occurs in many diverse ways; so will sin. Therefore, as a Church, it is vital that we learn to view the manifestation of sin, i.e.; spiritual strongholds; this way. Why? Because we are no more worthy of heaven than anyone described thus far. Yet there remains a hope for them that is largely predicated upon whether we as God's people can balance speaking out against sin while not discarding or turning our backs on the sinner. We can contend for truth and morality and should do so. We can also expose, resist and reject damaging liberal and secular influences - yet while always speaking truth in love to our opponent, with patience and gentleness as we have been called to do (2 Timothy 2:24-25).

I am reminded of Paul's letter to the Corinthians where he writes; "Do not be deceived: neither the sexually immoral, nor idolaters, nor adulterers, nor men who practice homosexuality, nor thieves, nor the greedy, nor drunkards, nor revilers, nor swindlers will inherit the kingdom of God. *And such were some of you.* But you were *washed*, you were *sanctified*, you were *justified*, in the name of the Lord Jesus Christ and by the Spirit of God" (1 Corinthians 6:9-11).

And that is the only difference between the Church of God and the stubborn atheist, the militant humanist, and even the sexually immoral and the transgendered. We have been graciously redeemed through no merit of our own, by no ability of our own, and for eternal plans and purposes that were not our own.

This is what I mean when I say that we all have a past resume before the grace received through salvation. None of us, no matter who we are, can claim to be any cleaner, or worthy of forgiveness and eternal life than our neighbors who are still lost, blind, and dead in trespasses and sins.

This country, our society, and the world we live in, as a whole, desperately needs God's people to reflect what we have received from Him and illuminate the spiritual darkness that is an intrinsic part of fallen and sinful mankind.

Therefore, as God's covenant body of people let us resolve to completely surrender ourselves unto Him while establishing our faith and focusing on Christ alone. May we likewise renew and solidify our commitment to Him who has entrusted to us the message of reconciliation and has thereby commissioned His redeemed as "ambassadors for Christ" in the midst of this fallen generation (2 Corinthians 5:19-20).

As vessels for His use, God works in and through us to impact our environment and accomplish His purposes. Thus, we are called to be spiritually sober, vigilant, and awake as we patiently await His promised return as our eternal and reigning King and the manifestation of Justice itself (Matthew 24:37-47, 25:31-46, 26:41, 1 Peter 1:13-19). Let's start preparing for that now.

We can begin by standing as a nation before God by first bending our knees to Him in prayer and repentance. Pray for Holy Spirit-led revival to sweep across our land. Pray for our country and its elected officials. Vote for political candidates who uphold biblical values and oppose the senseless murder of unborn babies and godless immorality that strikes against His design for life, marriage, and creation. Pray for wisdom, discernment, and conviction with reverence for God.

Let's work to promote discipleship studies for all age groups in our churches, particularly our youth, to help better prepare them for what they will encounter in college and this world in general. We need them to carry the message of the gospel forward, especially among their peers. They need us to learn more about God and the core essentials of the faith while better informing them of the plethora of ways this world oppresses it. We fall short if we allow them to enter this present-day society unaware and unprepared for the enemy who will seductively pull their attention away from God while simultaneously raking their faith over the coals. It is happening even now through the predominant societal philosophies that have swayed our children while gradually softening the Church's voice, presence, and influence in this country.

In contrast to this agenda; when we exhibit God's compassion, service, and love for sinners, yet without *compromising* His truth, through *conforming* to this world we live in (Romans 12:2), we then encourage and contribute to the growth and development of the church (and our nation) while fulfilling its purpose and mission on earth (Acts 17:30-31, Luke 24:46-47, Matthew 28:18-20).

In conclusion, as we seek to immerse our lives in His truth while maintaining necessary theocentric solidarity among us; we will then rightly navigate through this vast stream of opposing and damaging views, found everywhere within society today.

History and current events combine as substantial proof that humanistic thought and secular liberal philosophy have no place within the body of Christ. Not in the days of the early church, not in this present age, nor ever in the future.

May we stand together as God's redeemed and pray that His Holy Spirit will grant genuine revival and an increasing influence on the culture that surrounds us, and no longer the other way around.

Chapter 2 - We Belong Together

YOU WERE NOT DESIGNED TO live the Christian life, nor weather the tribulation encountered throughout this lifetime in isolation from other believers. In this spiritual battle you are in there are no lone soldiers or renegade warriors.

Just as a military platoon maximizes its strength and effectiveness from its discipline, organization, and numbers; so also are God's people the strongest when together in the unity of assembly. In fact, when we wander away from the congregation and seek to do things on our own we live in rejection of what God Himself has created for the nourishment and edification of His redeemed children. Instead of improving our circumstances or our spiritual condition, we put ourselves at even greater risk for decline. To remain intentionally separated from Christian worship and fellowship diminishes our ability to live for Christ, bear lasting fruit for His kingdom, or please our Savior with obedience. In addition, it outright denies the honor due Him while also greatly increasing the potential of spiritual attack from the enemy.

To belong to Christ comes with having an adversary who opposes God and His purposes. Satan desires to fight against the kingdom of God in every sense, and anyone who belongs to it. He prowls eagerly in search of a believer in a weakened state just as a hungry lion seeks out prey who have wandered away or been separated from the pack. His one desire is to steal, kill, and destroy (John 10:10a, 1 Peter 5:8). He is a stranger to mercy or compassion. Therefore, to live in willful detachment from the corporate "body" of Christ is to invite disaster and encourage spiritual shipwreck. Why do this? We become targets easily pursued by the enemy when we veer from the congregation in pursuit of independent Christian living. Furthermore, there is no biblical premise for us doing so. But more importantly, rejecting God's church is to spurn His design for His covenant body of people to the disgrace of His providence, and most especially, His Son who died for it.

The consensus of Scripture clearly reveals that God intends for His people to live in unity with one another and to work out whatever difficulties that may arise along the way (Matthew 18:15-16, Ephesians 4:1-6, 32; Philippians 2:1-4, 14-15). It is God's own design for us that we gather together to praise Him, worship Him, glorify His name, and attentively listen and obey the instruction from His Word. When this is combined with fellowship, acts of service, prayer, witnessing - we exhibit the design and function of

God's people as we model the intended out workings of the "body" of Christ, the church. In this sense, the church is neither a building nor a denomination as we may be accustomed to believing. In contrast, the church in its truest sense is the assembled body of God's chosen people who gather together in His name, for His glory, and in gratitude, for all He has done. As soldiers for the Lord, we receive our instruction here. We learn discipline and practice unity, self-sacrifice, and increased sanctification. The church is where we grow, mature, and develop as His covenant children in fellowship with Him. We are strongest when together. In sum, *we need each other.* Let us therefore utilize and embrace this means of grace that our God has provided at so great a cost and according to His eternal plan.

To live in willful separation from His church is contrary to His creative purposes. Just as Genesis 2:18 declares, "it is not good for the man to be alone;" likewise it is never good for the Christian believer to be alone apart from the body of Christ which *also* has been designed for our good and His glory (Ephesians 2:14-16, 3:6-12, 5:23, 25, 30; Matthew 16:18).

In the beginning, God created the first woman from man's side to be a loving, lifetime helper to him in the expression of God's grace and His power as Creator (Genesis 2:21-22). Equal in value and worth unto God yet distinct in role and function; the creation of woman provided compatible, covenantal relationships for man and this was God's providential means for propagating the human race throughout the ancient world. This still holds true today. In addition, man and woman are both gracious gifts from God and each is equally and essentially necessary to fully compliment the other. This is His design.

Just as man and woman spiritually become "one" in the union of biblical marriage, in a similar manner, the believer is likewise bonded in lasting spiritual union with God the Father, Son, and Holy Spirit through faith and the sovereign application of our redemption. As John Murray has noted, "In speaking of union with Christ and after comparing it with the union which exists between man and wife, Paul says: "This mystery is great, but I speak of Christ and of the church" (Ephesians 5:32).[6]

In other words, God's design for His creation and His church follow similar lines of purpose in terms of having a lasting covenant bond. Not only that, each covenant denotes a common thread of plurality and togetherness. Man is spiritually joined to woman through marital vows and the believer is joined in spiritual union with Christ through faith. Hence, when we were Sovereignly delivered "from the domain of darkness" and transferred into" the kingdom of His beloved Son" (Colossians 1:13-14) our salvation by God, likewise, ushered us directly into His eternal covenant body of people; the church. We are members of His "body" and are now connected to Him and one another based on the finished work

---

[6] Redemption Accomplished and Applied, John Murray (WM. B. Eerdmans 1955); pg 178

of Christ and in fulfillment of God's covenant design for His people. Thus, the Christian life is not one of separation but of connectivity. The fruit of which is expressed in corporate unity that functions according to God's plan and to His glory.

Just as woman was created for lasting union and intimacy with man, likewise the church was created for this eternal union and intimacy of His covenant body of believers. Moreover, as the covenantal nature of marriage has been God's purpose from the beginning of time to unite the handiwork of His creation, so the church always has been intended to be a permanent and intrinsic fabric woven into the life of every child of God; shared in union with others whom He has graciously called as His own (Ephesians 2:18-22, 3:3-6, 9-11; Colossians 1:24-26).

Interestingly, in the beginning, God the Father instructed our first ancestors to "be fruitful and multiply" in the propagation of the earth (Genesis 9:1); whereas God the Son tells His followers to go and "make disciples" of all nations, and as representatives of Him, to be fruitful and multiply the kingdom He has established on earth (Matthew 28:19, John 15:5, 8; 20:21). Therefore, salvation and unity consist to increase, never decrease. We are called to bond together as a church community, not separate into stark individuality.

Secondly, believers are part of the "body" of Christ in a spiritual sense, through our eternal union with Christ (Ephesians 2:19-21, 1 Corinthians 6:17); and we are quite obviously a part of His "body," the church, in the physical sense as well. The former is strengthened by the latter, but as already stated, there is never a willing separation of the two.

The corporate unity of the body is expressed throughout the New Testament. Hebrews 10:23-25 says, "Let us hold fast the confession of our hope without wavering, for he who promised is faithful. And let us consider how to stir up one another to love and good works, not neglecting to meet together, as is the habit of some, but encouraging one another, and all the more as you see the Day drawing near." The church congregation acting according to its function is a place of encouragement, focus, and godly counsel. We cling to our hope in faithful expectation of Christ's promises and His return. Contrary to being passive and inactive in doing so, we, instead, use our time together partly to urge one another forward in faith and endurance. We are to think of and consider how to "stir up one another to love and good works." Titus 2:13-14 reminds us that as God's people we are "waiting for our blessed hope, the appearing of our great God and Savior Jesus Christ, who gave himself for us to redeem us from all lawlessness and to purify for himself *a people for his own possession who are zealous for good works.*" We are His. Having been bought with a price, we are not our own – but are now "his own possession". We gather together in assembly as a congregation of the redeemed and we love one another as we patiently look forward in faith to the coming of our Savior (1 Corinthians 6:19, 1 John 3:1-3, Colossians 3:1-4). As one body we worship in unity as we grow in numbers and maturity.

This metaphor concerning the "body" is greatly exemplified by The Apostle Paul in his letter to the Corinthians. In his dissertation concerning the spiritual gifts, Paul, likewise, lends focus to the corporate unity that is characteristic of the church. 1 Corinthians 12:12, 14 says, "For just as the body is one and has many members, and all the members of the body, *though many, are one body,* so it is with Christ... For the body does not consist of one member but many." In a natural sense, our body is connected as one. Though many different parts exist individually, they are corporately joined together as a whole (Ephesians 2:21-22, 4:15-16, Romans 11:24). Paul's instruction regarding the spiritual gifts is that all are important, needed, and useful for the simple fact that each individual "member" contributes something to the corporate whole, the "body". So it is for all believers. God has gifted you in some way and your individual contribution and extension of your gift is indispensable to the other parts of His "body". God has designed it to be this way. "God arranged the members in the body, each one of them, as he chose" (1 Corinthians 12:18). There is to be no desertion and willful separation from that which He Himself has created. "If all were a single member, where would the body be? As it is, there are many parts, yet one body" (v19). We were not redeemed so that we would live in isolation. We need the strengthening, encouragement, and corporate unity of fellow believers. We all have something to share, and even the most simple acts of service have value. Paul summarizes this oneness, "If one member suffers, all suffer together; if one member is honored, all rejoice together" (v26). As corporate members of the body of Christ, we are spiritually joined and knitted together as one; in union with Him, and communion with one another.

It's clear that we are both needed and expected in church individually as well, for none of the above is possible if everyone took a leave of absence. The church is not expected to function upon the shoulder of a few faithful saints, but rather, collectively through the individual contribution of its members. If you are saved, this includes you. We are part of the church individually through faithful attendance, discovering and then using what spiritual gift God has imparted to us, also by sharing our testimony of what God has done for us, and in obedience to what Christ tells His disciples – to 'love one another' in unity.

The Westminster Confession of Faith writes, "All Saints, that are united to Jesus Christ, their head, by his Spirit, and by faith, have fellowship with him in his graces, sufferings, death, resurrection, and glory; and, being united together in love, they have communion in each other's gifts and graces, and are obliged to the performance of such duties, public and private..."[7]

---

[7]   The Westminster Confession of Faith, 26.1

Maybe this calls for a bit of self-sacrifice or extending mercy and forgiveness to someone, showing generosity, volunteering, leading or attending a Bible study, working as an usher or greeter, supporting missionaries, caring for children, thanking your pastor, donating to the church, singing in the choir – these are just some of the many ways an individual can contribute to their congregation and help to maintain the bond of peace within the church.

There are other forms of love and outreach, such as visiting the sick, elderly, and shut-ins. Some bring along in-house Bible studies, warm meals, needed supplies, and even do communion for those who are physically unable to attend church. Have you ever asked the Lord how you can make a difference? Are you willing to pray for opportunities to serve Him? What are some ways you can get active and be involved?

So often we are accustomed to viewing church as mere spectators and we assume that our role is something like being an extra in the audience. The truth is, church has little to do with the physical structure of a building; and it is certainly foreign to the concept of passive or subdued attendance. Instead, we need to think of church in terms of Christ as the Head, the Cornerstone, the Vine, and as our Good Shepherd. *This* is our commonality among one another and the reason why we come together as one. By faith, we look beyond what we see and we offer our worship, praise, prayer, and acts of service to Jesus who is the reason for it all. Without Christ, there is no cross. Without the cross, there is no church. Without the church and the presence of the Holy Spirit, there is no Christianity. When this reality penetrates the soul it becomes a catalyst that moves us into serving our Savior with humility and gratitude for the gift of salvation we have received through His amazing sacrifice.

We are fallen, sinful people who Jesus has called out by name (John 10:3, 14, 27). Our individual salvation comes connected to a corporate body of people who have likewise received His grace. Thus, our personal contributions to this 'body' are vital to its function, growth, unity, and overall effectiveness. The abundance of grace and mercy we have received through our union with Christ is not harbored deep within us to no avail but is meant to be distributed to those who are around us as vessels and conduits of His love. Our willingness to do this combined with our God-given individual giftedness affects the corporate whole of the church, and any environment that is outside of the church. It is in this sense that we are 'obliged to the performance of such duties, public and private.' Yet maybe difficulty, sadness, or other turmoil has caused us to drift from fellowship.

Even in suffering and affliction, your presence is needed in the church. Your faith, endurance, even your honest brokenness might encourage someone who is also going through a storm. It might stir up others in prayer or compassion. God can still work in and through you even in your toughest times. A worship song might be for you as He speaks comfort and assuredness. Or He might reach you in the message that's preached, or in something a brother or sister in Christ says. The simple fact we continue to come may encourage others to persevere while also showing that our tribulation is not the end of us. It does not have the final say. In our individual participation within the body of Christ, we exercise our union with Christ as well as our communion with others. We are needed there on the "good" days but also when things are not going well for us at all. Hope is shared and strengthened as we use this means of grace God has given to us, His "body", the church. To remain absent is contrary to what God Himself has designed and intended and we sacrifice much-needed nourishment in doing so.

Perhaps other influences have kept us away. Maybe we've never gone to church before, or have had a negative experience while attending one. Maybe we don't fully grasp its need in our life, or its overall design and function. Dr. Jon D. Payne notes, "Sadly, some doubt the importance of the church because they have been burned by unfaithful church leadership or wounded by a nasty church split. Others are tired of the hype and superficiality of consumeristic mega-churches. Still others, due to a deficiency of biblical knowledge, downplay or even reject the organization, authority, and ordinances of the church."[8] Many are still unaware

---

[8]   Dr. Jon D. Payne, Table Talk, February 2018, pg50

of its design and function, nor understand their need for it or their personal role within it. These wide ranges of possibilities further underscore the need to discuss and define these ramifications while also clarifying a biblical foundation from which to proceed in establishing a right view concerning the church, without which it is easy to create unhelpful and unscriptural ideas and practices while living in separation from the body of Christ. But as Dr. Payne observes, "Christians are never stronger in isolation from the faithful ministry of the local church. The organized church is God's idea."[9]

Contrary to the "me"-focused culture we live in and the relativism so prevalent in the world today, we are God's chosen covenant people who belong to Him and are now part of His "body," the Church. Establishing a correct view concerning it is vitally important if we are to obey and honor Him rightly while exercising this means of grace He has provided also for our edification and sanctification The aim in view is that we would then come to see our need for, and role within the corporate assembly of what God Himself has created and ordained for those who belong to Him.

---

[9]   Dr. Payne, Table Talk

Chapter 3 - The Intimacy of The Church

THROUGH THE APOSTLE PAUL, THE Holy Spirit explicitly reveals "Christ loved the Church and gave himself for her" (Ephesians 5:25). He sacrificed Himself willingly for us, for His own body of believers, His sheep, His elect, His beloved children who are now co-Heirs with Him. Think about that for a moment. As a believer, you are a *co-heir* with Christ Jesus. God, our Father, has chosen to include His children in His heavenly kingdom upon the merits of His Son. We have been graciously included in this eternal blessing! In Christ, all that is rightfully His becomes our own. This is what it means to be a co-heir with Christ (Romans 8:17, Galatians 3:29, Titus 3:4-7). As God's adopted children, we have the future hope of this divine inheritance because of the Lord's sacrificial death, burial, and resurrection for His people.

Because of God's great mercy, you have been born again to a living hope that is anchored upon the resurrection of Jesus Christ from the grave. Your eternal life, made possible by His death, now connects you to an inheritance that is described as imperishable, undefiled, unfading, kept in heaven *for you* (1 Peter 1:3-5). God's gracious love is intimately applied through the effectual call of the sinner to Himself (John 6:37-40), while all His spiritual blessings are thereby rendered to those who at that time become a member of His body, the Church, and a co-heir to Christ and His heavenly kingdom. The Westminster Confession of Faith informs us that this assembly of people that Christ loved and died for "...consists of the whole number of the elect, that have been, are, or shall be gathered into one, under Christ..."[10] One scholar rightly adds, "The visible church on earth is a society of believing and holy persons, whom God, by the gospel, has called from among mankind, to fellowship with his Son Jesus Christ."[11] In other words, your personal salvation that was fully known and ordained by the Godhead in eternity became manifested in your life in the moment of belief (which itself was a gift of God) through the gospel, numbering you personally among His very own, in fellowship and union with Christ forever in a covenant relationship that will never end. It is personal in that, Jesus speaks of "*His* Church."[12] It is intimate and binding in that the

---

[10] The Westminster Confession of Faith, 25.1

[11] Systematic Theology, by John Brown of Haddington (Reformation Heritage Books, 2015) pg 551

[12] Biblical Theology, by Geerhardus Vos (Banner of Truth 2014) pg 400

Apostle Paul likens this bond, this covenant, with the ordinance of marriage where two "become one flesh" (Ephesians 5:31b). He declares that as believers "we are members of his body" (Ephesians 5:30), and that "Christ is the head of the church, his body, and is himself its Savior" (Ephesians 5:23). This union, this covenant that exists between us is a gracious gift, a God-designed ordinance, and a spiritual blessing associated with our salvation.

We are His own people who were redeemed by Him personally, savingly, and eternally. John Calvin once said. to those to whom God is a Father, the Church must also be a "mother." We receive faith, growing and sustaining nourishment there. The Greek word 'ecclesia' (which is rendered 'church' in the New Testament) denotes an assembly of God's redeemed children. Ecclesia simply means a group of people called out from something. In reference to the church, it means a gathering together of people who have been called out from this world to serve God. We have been brought from darkness into the light (Ephesians 5:8), set free from the bondage of sin and death (Romans 6:20-23). As God's children, we have been made spiritually alive (Ephesians 3:1), having been delivered *out of* the domain of darkness and transferred *into* the kingdom of God's beloved Son (Colossians 1:13). Like Lazarus, we also have been called out of the tomb of sin, death, and decay (John 11:43-44). Like Samuel, the Lord has called us into service for His sake. Like Daniel, we have been called to remain faithful to Him in the midst of a sinful and pagan environment. Like Zaccheus, we have been called by name out of the sycamore tree. Like Paul, we have been shown the light of Jesus Christ and were redirected from our own wayward road to Damascus. Like Lydia, our hearts have been opened by God to receive His truth. Like the man who was blind since birth, He has given us the eyes to see Jesus beyond just a teacher, prophet, or some kind of humanitarian worker – but as a personal Savior who knows us by name and who calls to follow Him and to reign with Him in future glory. Our grave clothes were traded for the righteousness of Christ (2 Corinthians 5:21), our sin was replaced with His salvation (Titus 3:3-7), with our iniquities blotted out (Psalm 51:9, Isaiah 43:25, 44:22), we have been washed as white as snow (Psalm 51:7, Isaiah 1:18). As the writer of Hebrews tells us, "Therefore let us be grateful for receiving a kingdom that cannot be shaken, and thus let us offer to God acceptable worship, with reverence and awe" (Hebrews 12:28).

A church is a group of people who belong to God. In humility and gratitude, we give our lives to Him for all that He is and all He has done. We turn *from* the things of this world and the darkness we once knew and we turn *to* God to serve Him with love and appreciation all the days of our lives. That's what church is. We are people who have been called out, and we gather together to worship Him for this grace we have received and to praise Him for our salvation. We come to hear the Word of God by which our faith came and grows and in our sanctification we seek to increasingly obey it and conform our lives to it.

Furthermore, we participate in the sacraments, which the Lord instituted before His sacrificial death, the Lord's Supper, and Baptism. We have fellowship with other believers who are part of this covenant family as we pray for and encourage one another to reflect our Father, mature in our faith, strengthen each other, make disciples, and witness to a lost and dying world. Do you see how this would honor God and why this would be His design for His people? Can you sense here why our attendance is encouraged as well as necessary? Dr. Payne adds the following observation: "It is through, not apart from, the ministry of the church that Christ and His benefits are efficaciously communicated to the elect and received through faith. A serious Christian, then, does not craft a mosaic of personalized spirituality outside the church. No, true faith believes Christ's promise to feed His sheep through the faithful ministry of a biblical church."[13] Our union with Christ includes the fact we are now members of His body, chosen, sanctified, and set apart by Him and for Him (Ephesians 5:27). Paul refers to 'the household of God" (1 Timothy 3:15). It is where our "faith might be nourished."[14] To shun this and to reject our involvement with the church "is denial of God

---

[13] Dr. Payne, Table Talk

[14] The Institutes of The Christian Religion, by John Calvin (Hendrickson 2008) 4.1.5, pg 675

and Christ."[15] How so? It is because our union is that personal and that intimate with Him and because the church is God's design for His covenant assembly of people. Dr. Payne continues, "The Bible everywhere assumes that believers will be vitally connected to the church. The sacraments of baptism and the Lord's Supper powerfully reinforce the Christian's union and communion with Christ and fellow believers. Not only is it God's purpose for us to mature under the shepherding care and faithful ministry of the church, but also to build one another up in love."[16] We will explore the three critical marks that distinguish a true church momentarily, but for now, notice here how our attendance and participation are instrumental for our growth as Christians: God ministers to His people through His pastors, His sacraments, and the unity among His people in fellowship and worship.

To be part of the Church is to be part of God's own family. It is to hear from our Father and worship our Lord and Savior together as *co-heirs* with Christ by the power of the Holy Spirit who strengthens our faith and causes us to grow in the image and likeness of God's Son (Romans 8:29). This was God's design for His covenant body of people whom He personally foreknew, predestined, called, justified, and glorified according to His eternal plan and purposes (Romans 8:30).

---

[15] Calvin, Institutes 4.1.9, pg 679

[16] Dr. Payne, Table Talk

Paul writes to the Ephesians that believers were chosen in Christ before the foundation of this world. "In love, God has predestined us for adoption as sons according to the purpose of His will, to the praise of His glorious grace, with which He has blessed us in the beloved" (Ephesians 1:4-6). Moreover, we have been washed and redeemed of our iniquities, bought with a price, and spared from God's wrath and judgment against sin. How did He do this? One by one He has called us by name. This is how Christ "loved the church and gave Himself up for her (Ephesians 5:25b). How are we loving Him in return?

Chapter 4 - What The Church Looks Like

PAUL URGES US TO WALK with "all humility and gentleness, with patience, bearing with one another in love, eager to maintain the unity of the Spirit in the bond of peace" (Ephesians 4:2-3). One scholar has rightly noted this timeless fact: "True unity is accomplished when people love one another." [17] Love conjures up ideas of closeness, sacrifice, and mutual affection. We could also include the desire to make things work. Love conquers and it overcomes obstacles. It tears down walls, defuses hostility, and forgives. Is this easy to do at all times? Not hardly, there can be difficulty that comes with it as many have experienced. We must remember, "Jesus Christ died, intercedes and bestows his Spirit and grace, in order to promote the unity and peace of his church." [18] Again, we are called to be "eager to maintain the unity of the Spirit in the bond of peace." Puritan, John Brown,

---

[17]   Ephesians – An Exegetical Commentary, by Harold Hoehner (Baker)

[18]   Systematic Theology, John Brown, pg 556

rightly said; "The union and communion of the Christian church is of *great importance*. True believers being, by the inviolable bonds of the Spirit and faith, connected with Christ as their head, and with their fellow-saints as one with him, there can be no schism in, or separation from his invisible church, or mystical body."[19] We are to avoid any such thing, as these are contrary to unity itself and Christian living altogether. "Schism" being defined as "uncharitableness and alienation of affection among church members, who, in the main, continue in church fellowship with one another."[20] or worse yet, when it causes separation and desertion of the church altogether. Coldness between church members can creep in like someone leaving the window open during the middle of the winter. Over time, a chill replaces the warmth of the room. What comfort previously existed, evaporates by the dominating presence of cold. Unfortunately, this sometimes happens within the congregation. In some sense, it should be somewhat expected. By that I mean, we are a group of redeemed sinners all under one roof. Each person is not at the same level of understanding or maturity. Moreover, we do not all share the same besetting sin and therefore there is a plethora of personal malfunctioning that is possible. What is an area of strength for one person might be an area of weakness for another. This melting pot of personalities, differences, and characteristics can

---

[19] Systematic Theology, John Brown, pg 553

[20] Systematic Theology, John Brown, pg 555

sometimes boil over if not closely monitored and then mediated on with both prayer and forgiveness. Hence we should be making every effort to encourage, maintain, and contribute to the spiritual warmth of our church. To allow coldness to continue and by feeding into schisms that surface among the members, we become not vessels for Christ but welcome tools used by the enemy. What appears to you to be a personal issue on the surface, has deeper spiritual significance than you may realize. The devil finds room to work within the church when believers yield not to humility and unity but insist on drawing lines of separation because of personal differences or grievances, none of which will follow us into our eternal home. He who sacrificed, forgave, and was an instrument of peace now calls us to do the same (Luke 17:3-4, Matthew 18:27, Ephesians 4:32). As He tells His disciples in the Sermon on the Mount: "Blessed are the peacemakers, for they shall be called the sons of God" (Matthew 5:9). Peace maintains both warmth and unity.

Division within the church is typically caused by "pride, self-love, jealousy, hatred, evil-speaking, etc. It ought to be prevented by self-denial, taking up our cross and exact the following of Christ."[21] One great Puritan once spoke of the church likened to many different branches of all different lengths, thicknesses, some with bends, some straighter, all very different in appearance and types. To go and

---

[21] Systematic Theology, John Brown, pg 555

collect such a wide assortment of branches like this would be difficult to carry in your hands. But if you were to lay down a length of cord and wrap it around the branches, bound together now, you could quite easily carry them to your destination. In the same way, God's Holy Spirit has taken all of us and has bound us together in unity in the bond of peace and we are to avoid schism and division, and instead, be eager to maintain what the Spirit has accomplished. In this way we honor God, obey what He has said, and help one another greatly, as we head to our heavenly destination together. There is no place for coldness, pettiness, separation, or division in the body of Christ. It is contrary to all that we profess to be. Jonathon Edwards so aptly summarizes it this way: "An envious Christian, a malicious Christian, a cold-hearted Christian, is the greatest absurdity and contradiction. It's as if one speaks of dark brightness or false truth."[22]Jesus tells us, "This is My commandment, that you love one another as I have loved you" (John 15:12). He says, "If you love Me, you will keep[23] My commandments." (John 14:15). "Whoever has My commandments and keeps them, he it is who loves Me. And he who loves Me will be loved by my Father, and I will love him and manifest Myself to him" (John 14:21). Love is the catalyst

---

[22] Religious Affection, Jonathon Edwards (Banner of Truth)

[23] The word "keep" in this verse is in the Present tense, indicating *ongoing* obedience in the believer's life to that which Jesus has commanded us.

of unity. Unity is united togetherness. Though differences may exist, the common foundation our lives are built upon should greatly outweigh it all. Who are we to excuse ourselves from His "body?" It is God's own design for His Church that believers assemble and dwell in unity.

Herein we affect our environment and the church in the ways that our God has intended. Jesus tells His followers, "You are the light of the world. A city set on a hill cannot be hidden. Nor do people light a lamp and put it under a basket, but on a stand, and it gives light to the entire house. In the same way, let your light shine before others, so that they may see your good works and give glory to your Father who is in heaven" (Matthew 5:14-16).

Light emits and radiates outward thus warming and illuminating the surrounding areas to the benefit of others. It expels darkness. One single candle flame has a noticeable effect on any room that is absent of light. In this sense, followers of Christ are to have a noticeable presence in the environments we find ourselves in, whether in the assembly or outside of the church. Not that we ourselves stand out or somehow command attention from others, but rather, as we increasingly submit to this Light who is *already within us* Christ then shines forth in our thoughts, words, and actions. He is thereby recognizable to others – and, to the glory of the Father (John 8:12, 14:6, 15:8; Ephesians 5:8). This is our purpose. It's what we are called to do. As once empty and broken vessels, we are now filled with the

Holy Spirit to reflect God's light, love, mercy, and forgiveness.

Knitted together within the body of Christ, we are vitally connected to Jesus as a branch is to the vine (John 15:5). Without Him, we can do *nothing*. Grafted in through the gracious act of salvation, we now belong with others who are also united to Christ through faith. As we begin to bear fruit for Him and His kingdom, we reveal to the world around us the "light" that is the answer to their every need.

Attending services and participating in the assembly is the natural outworking of being united to Christ in salvation while simultaneously being knit to one another in love. Peace, love, and light maintain the warmth and unity that are necessary and essential characteristics of God's church while also accurately reflecting its purposes to others, both inside and outside of the covenant congregation. This is what the church was created to look like. In our actions and attitudes, we either contribute to the building up or the tearing down of God's plan, purposes, and people.

Before moving on there is one final point to make that is entirely necessary regarding the 'unity' of God's church. What has been described thus far is quite essential as well as thematically correct. Nevertheless, there remain nuances to unity that I believe would be irresponsible not to explain, to you the reader. Furthermore, I am inclined to do so because up to this point in the discussion it would be easy for someone to assume that we are to cast off all distinctions and overlook essential doctrinal matters for the sake of amassing one universal congregation. But that is not the unity we have in mind here, nor is it the view Jesus or the Apostles held. In contrast, the goal and vision of the church are for unity that is founded in truth, love, and our common mission as His body of disciples. Rightfully so, orthodox Christianity *is* distinct from some of the existing cults who, on the surface, appear to be a part of the faith. Yet a closer look at groups, like the Jehovah's Witnesses and the Mormons, reveal distortions to Scripture, church history, and the essentials concerning who and what our faith is based upon.[24] In addition, we are vastly different and distinct from the popular New Age spirituality and Eastern Mysticism; both of which teach forms of Gnosticism, polytheism, and pantheism. These, in brevity, translate into a secret "knowledge" that rejects the doctrine of sin and believes that true enlightenment to a higher state of consciousness can only be obtained by a small number of spiritual humanity; at times in conjunction with the belief of numerous mythological deities and the idea that God exists in the spirit of mountains, trees, and resides within all created and inanimate things.

Though cults and other groups may advocate and model both love and witnessing to others, the details in their system of belief, differ greatly from

---

[24] For further detail concerning these groups, and others, the author suggests consulting The Kingdom of the Cults by Walter Martin (Nelson Publishers).

that which was "once for all delivered to the saints" (Jude 3b). Love for self, independence, and the propagation of false teachings hardly align with the goals or mission of God's church, regardless of any perceived area of similarity. Therefore, distinctions, differences, and core essential doctrines[25] are in every sense necessary to help separate us from the counterfeit and the imposters.

Yet, even within Christianity, some varieties of differences exist. Here it is important that we don't major in the minors. In other words, let us not create unnecessary and lasting division over non-essentials. For example, you might believe differently concerning when a person should be baptized, the kind of worship music that should be used, or how a person is or is not able to come to salvation in the Lord. We can disagree on these points, but guess what? I still love you as my brother or sister in Christ. We can still share in God's love, His truth, and His mission for the church. We are family. We have the same Father. Though certain particulars might have us established in this or that denomination, *we remain unified as a whole.*

Consider, by way of illustration; the United States military. There is the Army, Navy, Air Force, Marines, and Coast Guard. Each branch is distinct. They all have different uniforms, there are variations in rank, they assemble at different

---

[25] See the Appendix for a Confession of Faith which cities these necessary specifics and distinctions.

bases, plus other idiosyncratic details; yet with one unified purpose and overall mission that they follow. Moreover, they all fall under the leadership of our U.S. government and Commander in Chief; the President.

Likewise, true Christian denominations are also like a branch of the military. Denominations are distinct. There often exist subtle differences. We assemble in a variety of churches. Nevertheless, though distinct from one another, we have a unified purpose for God's overall mission on earth. Additionally, I believe it fair to say that we all have some understanding of our role and responsibility within the congregation as well as to the world that is outside its doors. But more than that, if we are born-again believers who depend on the authority of God's Word and are built upon the cornerstone of Jesus Christ and all that He has taught us, *without* compromising it, redefining it, or watering it down to appease an increasingly godless and liberal society; then regardless of certain small, non-essential distinctions which might exist between us, collectively speaking – we still faithfully acknowledge and submit to the Sovereign headship of Christ as His very own body of people, the church (Colossians 1:18, Ephesians 1:22-23).

Therefore, unity with distinction can co-exist. In fact, our model and the example we are to follow is the Trinity itself. By that, I mean God the Father, God the Son, and God the Holy Spirit are united in truth, love, and mission. Moreover, each member is intrinsically equal in divine essence and being, yet they are distinct in their role and function, though still one. Consider the following:

God the Father is primarily regarded as Creator, Covenant maker, and Sovereign elector. God the Son is largely distinguished as Savior, Redeemer, Mediator, covenant Head, our substitutionary and atoning sacrifice, and the accomplisher of our redemption. God the Holy Spirit is similarly distinct in His various roles of Comforter, Sanctifier, and the one who enlightens our minds to God's truth, applying salvation to our hearts, and sealing us with His indwelling presence. These are just a fraction of the differences but this should suffice to show that unity does not dissolve distinction. Rather, *just as they* are united in truth, love, and mission - *we* are now called to do the same (John 17:20-21).

Paul's letter to the Ephesians helps us understand how this is done. Following his pastoral exhortation for believers to walk in humility, gentleness, and patience; Paul now cites the spiritual gifts that are given by Christ to His church 'to equip the saints for the work of ministry." These gifts are for the express purpose of "building up the body of Christ." Additionally, there is a perpetual nature to this edification "until we attain to the unity of faith and the knowledge of the Son of God" (Ephesians 4:1-13a). In other words, as His church, we are to utilize what He has provided for us and grow stronger together in single-mindedness regarding

God's Word, God's love, and God's ministry in reaching the world. Not only that, but we are to progressively mature in all three aspects as a spiritual body that receives its instruction and sustenance from Christ, as we increasingly conform our lives to Him while we faithfully and expectantly await His glorious return. *This* is the 'unity' we are to strive for and maintain.

Distinction and differences will follow us all the way to heaven. The book of Revelation tells us there will be a great multitude that no one could number, "from *every nation*, from all *tribes* and *peoples* and *languages*," standing before the throne and before the Lamb, clothed in white robes, with palm branches in their hands, and crying out in a loud voice, "Salvation belongs to our God who sits on the throne, and to the Lamb!" (Revelation 7:9). We need not run from distinction or attempt to construct a one-world congregation.

In conclusion, denominations and our historic confessions of faith (see Appendix) have their necessary place as do Christian doctrinal essentials which help separate us from cults who deny the Deity of Christ, distort God's truth, and are founded on man-made religion far from the faith once for all delivered to the saints.

As God's covenant children, the body of Christ, we are called to stand firm on our foundation, our Cornerstone of faith and commonality. Because when God's people unite around the truth of His inspired Word, love one another as He loves us, and work together for the common purpose of ministry, outreach, and the building up of the body of Christ – we reveal to the world the glory of the Father, the beauty of the Son, and the presence of the Holy Spirit. That's unity with distinction.

Chapter 5 - What Distinguishes The Church

SO, WHAT THEN DISTINGUISHES A "true church?" Historically, it has been observed that three critical marks define a biblical church: 1) the pure preaching of the gospel 2) the right administration of the sacraments 3) the proper exercise of Christian discipline."[26]

We could further add that such preaching of the Word of God might include "explaining his law and gospel, and pointing his truths in the most particular manner to the consciences of hearers, for their conviction, conversion, sanctification, and comfort."[27] This should be done by those who are "duly qualified and called to that work"[28] (2 Corinthians 3:5-6, 2 Timothy 2:2, Ephesians 4:11-13, Romans 10:15). Sound preaching should aim to "exalt Christ, humble man, and bring them

---

[26] The Heidelberg catechism, Lord's Day 31, Questions 83-84

[27] Systematic Theology, John Brown, pg 519

[28] Systematic Theology, John Brown, pg 519

to God in Christ."[29] All of this, to the glory of God and in faithfulness to that calling, and to His Word. May His ministers also seek to speak clearly, always scriptural, and faithful "giving to saints and sinners that which best answers their diversified states and circumstances ... wisely, the doctrine and manner of delivering it being suited to the capacities and the circumstances of the hearers."[30]

This list is not meant to be fully exhaustive, but rather, provide you with some idea of what you should be looking for. Pure preaching should be God-breathed, God-centered, and God-motivated. Note also that varying degrees of purity will be found. Some churches will be very biblical in what they both teach and do, while others may not resemble a church at all. The Westminster Confession of Faith notes, "The purest churches under heaven are subject both to mixture and error; and some have so degenerated, as to become no churches of Christ, but synagogues of Satan. Nevertheless, there shall always be a church on earth, to worship God according to His will."[31] We will not find absolute perfection here on earth but shall find a place of worship that seeks to honor and fulfill God's function for His Church. Calvin adds, "when we say that the pure ministry of the Word and pure celebration of the sacraments

---

[29] Systematic Theology, John Brown, pg 519

[30] Systematic Theology, John Brown, pg 519

[31] The Westminster Confession of Faith, 25.5

is a fit pledge and earnest, so that we may safely recognize a church in every society in which both exist, our meaning is, that we are never to discard it so long as those remain, though it may otherwise teem with other faults."[32] Our culture today is accustomed to shopping around at a whim but with no intent of loyalty. To leave a church for personal and petty reasons is based solely on selfishness. Consider the issues going on in the church of the Corinthians and the Galatians, yet the Apostle Paul never advised anyone to bail out. Undoubtedly, the three distinguishing marks of a church were still present even among its many difficulties Paul's apostolic authority is biblically confirmed. Apollos and Cephas are likewise cited as teachers to the Corinthians. Therefore, there is support for a **distinguishing mark (1)** being present in the church (1 Corinthians 1:1-9, 23)**. Distinguishing mark (2)** the Lord's Supper was being administered; albeit imperfectly at the time (1 Corinthians 11:17-34). I am convinced Paul's rebuke and instruction corrected this particular problem. Finally, a **distinguishing mark (3)** is explicitly revealed in (1Corinthians 5:1-13), then finding its resolution and restoration in (2 Corinthians 2:5-11). *It seems as though issues were effectively admonished, disciplined, and dealt with as the Word of God was faithfully preached and the sacraments administered.* May we also learn to persevere through various difficulties

---

[32] Calvin, Institutes 4.1.12, pg 681

within the body of Christ, and if able, contribute positively and productively to the repentance and resolution of them. The Westminster Confession of Faith teaches, "Saints, by profession, are bound to maintain a holy fellowship and communion in the worship of God, and in performing such other spiritual services as tend to their mutual edification…"[33] Calvin wisely summarizes the issue, "it is vain to look for a church all together free from blemish."[34] It is neither biblical nor realistic for us to seek a church that is completely perfect here on earth nor to excuse ourselves from the assembly until we reach true perfection in heaven. The Church is God's design for His covenant assembly of redeemed people. Let us do our part to obey our Lord and honor this ordinance that was enacted by His love, sacrifice, and suffering – for our sake. We are now, and will always be, members of His "body." May our worship, praise, attendance, fellowship, and willing service resonate with this temporal and eternal fact.

Before we continue to the second and third distinguishing marks of a true church, I think it is important at this point to address the issue of false brethren before moving on. It is true in almost any setting that not all who are in the congregation are born again children of God. People go to church for many different reasons. Some are traditionalists

---

[33] The Westminster Confession of Faith, 26.2

[34] Calvin, Institutes 4.1.13, pg 681

who attend because their family always has, or it's just "the thing to do" on Sunday. Some go for business reasons, perhaps to network and such. Others may go to appease a loved one or are instead driven by guilt, or perhaps have a form of religion and are in a sense simply going through the motions of church.

Yes, Christ did warn that the church would be made up of a body of both wheat and tares (Matthew 13:24-30). Some people are still unregenerate yet are being drawn by Christ unto their eventual salvation, which is very good and also likely in some cases. Some are not and instead may appear outwardly good while being inwardly deceitful, fallen, and corrupt. We shouldn't strain to scrutinize critically and thus raise ourselves onto His throne of judgment. Remember that we are certainly called to exercise wise discernment in our dealings with people both in and out of the body of Christ (Matthew 7:6, 15-20, 33-35; Proverbs 1:10, 2:6, 14:7, 16) while trusting God that at the harvest He will indeed tell the reapers, "Gather the *weeds* first and bind them in bundles to be burned, but gather the *wheat* into my barn" (Matthew 13:30). Christ advised His disciples to "Let both grow together until the harvest… lest in gathering the weeds you root up the wheat along with them" (Matthew 13:29-30). None of us are to tolerate rampant wickedness within the Church. This is yet another reason why we need pure preaching and loving discipline with a focus on repentance, restoration, and if deemed necessary, even removal (Matthew 18: 15-20, 1 Corinthians 5: 1-13). God will someday rightly correct that which we cannot. In the meantime, however, we are to rightly act in accord with the wisdom, commands, and means of grace He has provided us.

For those who are more discerning and mindful of the disparity which exists between either true and false brethren and/or mature and weak ones, Calvin wisely instructs "mercifully correct what they can, and to bear patiently with what they cannot, in love lamenting and mourning until either God reforms or corrects, or at the harvest roots up the tares, and scatters the chaff."[35] He certainly will. Again, He has promised to do this very thing. For us, if our concentration were on the preaching of His Word and the participation of His sacraments while lovingly fellowshipping with the other congregants we shall then remain obedient to the Lord as we seek to serve Him rightly and reflect His presence wholly in our lives. This will accumulate over time and manifest in our life as we reserve all that remains to His care. May our worship, obedience, praise, service, integrity, zeal, and fortitude be used by God to admonish the idle and to convict the ingenuine among us. But we must not excuse ourselves from faithful attendance of the assembly merely because of noted imperfections within it.

---

[35] Calvin, Institutes 4.1.16 pg 682

Our Sovereign King and Judge will effectively and eternally separate that which does not belong to Him (Matthew 7: 21-23, 13: 30, 49-50; 22: 11-14, 25: 11-12, 31-46). Calvin reminds us that in our own estimating of the church, the "divine is of more force than human judgment."[36]

In conclusion, the pure preaching of the Gospel will constructively edify His body and prepare His people to respond faithfully, obediently, and correctly to issues that arise within the church. In addition, effective biblical preaching is blessed by God's Holy Spirit to usher conviction to the sinful and wayward while strengthening and encouraging the faithful and fruitful among us. In this way, this first distinguishing mark concerning the pure preaching of the Gospel works as an obvious antidote to the spread of sin within the body of Christ while simultaneously edifying members toward good works and faithful living. The second distinguishing mark of a true church is the right administration of the sacraments. What sacraments? These that the Lord Himself has instituted. Not Rome, not the Pope, not the priest – but Christ alone. There are two: The Lord's Supper (Matthew 26: 26-29, Mark 14: 22-24, Luke 22: 14-20, 1 Corinthians 11: 23-26), and Baptism (Matthew 28: 18-20, Acts 2:38, 8: 29, 34-39). They are given to the Church for its progressive sanctification, edification, and continued communion with the Lord.

---

[36] Calvin, Institutes 4.1.16 pg 683

<u>The Lord's Supper</u>

The Westminster Confession of Faith tells us, "Our Lord Jesus, in the night wherein he was betrayed, instituted the sacrament of his body and blood, called the Lord's Supper, to be observed *in his church*, unto the end of the world for the perpetual remembrance of the sacrifice of himself in his death…"[37]

The fact this sacrament was instituted by Jesus before His death and left His church that He died for should in itself highlights the importance of our corporate participation in this event. It is a distinguishing mark of a true church, and a true disciple, to obey what Jesus has said in regard to this sacrament. "*Do this* in remembrance of Me" (1 Corinthians 11: 23-26, Luke 22: 17-20).

Christ gave the Lord's Supper to His disciples primarily for the remembrance of what our salvation cost Him. We are to reflect on this before partaking in the sacrament. The beating and the horrible crucifixion He experienced for our sake are symbolized by the bread and wine, which symbolically represent the body and blood of Christ (John 6: 48-58). No one has suffered or sacrificed for you as Jesus did. It is hugely important and sanctifying to partake of the Lord's Supper and to "remember" what He did for you and in your place. His body was broken and His blood was poured out *for you.* And so, in this sense, we are to think back to the **past** as we

---

[37] The Westminster Confession of Faith, 29.1

remember Christ's sacrifice and substitution for our sins on Calvary. 2000 years ago the Son of God hung naked on the cross and died in your place as your substitute. Without Christ, there is no salvation from God's wrath, judgment, hell, and eternal separation from Him. Consider this as you reflect on the nature of His suffering and death that vividly demonstrate to mankind the filth, corruption, and costly nature of our sins. To remember this helps keep us sharp and vigilant at confessing and removing any known sin in our lives while also striving to prevent it from lingering in our life unattended.

But we tend to forget this part of Christianity. We'd prefer to focus on blessings and promises. These have their time and place. But as we initially 'remember' the Lord's great sacrifice on our behalf; this entails his bloodiness and brokenness for our sake. Remember His pain, suffering – and His loving willingness to do all of this for you. As a result, thank Him for His perfect obedience and righteousness, which were both imputed to you in salvation.

Therefore, let us never lose sight of the cross. It is a timeless centerpiece of Christian faith. Some today wish to minimize it or water down its importance. Some leave it out altogether in hopes of moving past this bloody yet historical part of Christianity. But true disciples of the Lord 'remember' it all in humble gratitude for this brutal and loving sacrifice. The Lord's Supper gives us the opportunity to receive His grace afresh and meditate on its vast significance in our lives. We do this, as He has instructed His church; in remembrance of Him.

The Lord's Supper is also a time to reflect right now in the **present** of our election, redemption, justification, union with Christ, adoption by God, our sanctification – all of these because of Him, for us. The Lord's Supper is a time of remembrance and reflection of Christ's finished work and what He has graciously accomplished and provided. Calvin wisely adds, "Having become with us the Son of Man, he has made us with himself sons of God. By his own descent to the earth, he has prepared our ascent to heaven. Having received our mortality, he has bestowed on us immortality. Having undertaken our weakness, he has made us strong in his strength. Having submitted to our poverty, he has transferred to us his riches. Having taken upon himself the burden of unrighteousness."[38] In this way, the Lord's Supper is a sacrament to be celebrated in grateful recognition of our Lord and Savior who has provided bountifully more than sometimes we even realize. As His church, we both corporately and individually "remember" that at this time.

Sin is a plague that affects us all. To be in Christ is to have been cured of the penalty of this debilitating disease. In this way, Jesus "took on our infirmities.' We've been chosen, redeemed, justified, sanctified, and have eternal union with the Godhead. *Remember this*. As you transition your thoughts from the event

---

[38] Calvin, Institutes 4.17.2 pg's 896-897

of the cross itself to the spiritual blessings which were poured forth because of it, thank him now for all He has so richly provided in salvation.

As Calvin noted; Jesus became, did, and provided all we would ever need while simultaneously giving us an abundance of gifts and riches no one could ever deserve or merit. In this way, the Lord's Supper becomes a graceful catalyst for celebrating our present status in Christ in remembrance of all his finished work entails.

In addition, the Lord's Supper further includes a wonderful, promising, and encouraging look to the *future* as we look forward to our reunion with Him, and the Marriage Supper of the Lamb (Revelation 19: 6-9, Luke 14: 15). Yes, "Blessed is everyone who will eat bread in the kingdom of God!" We who will someday reign with Him in eternity (2 Timothy 2:12, Revelation 20: 6) look forward to the glorious appearing of our Lord to consummate our redemption in Him and live in His presence forever (1 John 3: 1-3, Colossians 3: 1-4, 1 Corinthians 15: 53-58). The Apostle Paul instructs us, "our citizenship is in heaven, and from it, we await a Savior, the Lord Jesus Christ, who will transform our lowly body to be like his glorious body, by the power that enables him even to subject all things to himself" (Philippians 3: 20-21). Death has lost its sting (1 Corinthians 15: 55). We now eagerly look forward to incorruptible bodies and a perfect, sinless, and eternal environment that has been divinely prepared for us. Even king David could rightly say, "Surely goodness and mercy shall follow me all the days of my life, *and I shall dwell in the house of the Lord forever.*" (Psalm 23: 6)

In this sacrament, we have much to be thankful for and to "remember" **past, present, and future**. It was given to us for our good and his glory. As God's children, we are invited to His table. It is both unwise and disrespectful to spurn so great an offer (Matthew 22: 1-14).

Finally, we must remember that we are also called to inward self-examination prior to partaking in the Lord's Supper, lest we eat and drink of it unworthily (1 Corinthians 11: 28-29). Keep in mind this sacrament is not only for those who walk faithful and upright. It is also for them who struggle against sin and fall short – yet are genuinely concerned and repentant of it. It is for people who recognize their sincere dependency on the Father, Son, and Holy Spirit in salvation and sanctification. You must be a believer, and you must not be practicing a sinful lifestyle. It is not to say that we will not sin, but rather, if you simply give up your resistance to fighting sin and you make a willful practice of it, and you are walking in sin – it is best not to participate in the Lord's Supper until that is fully resolved. Lifestyles that are characterized by sin are enemies to Christ. To partake of this sacrament at this point would not be celebrating it, but mocking it instead. "Examine yourselves, test yourselves" to see whether you are in the faith" (2 Corinthians 13: 5).

In your self-examination, ask yourself; do you *love* Christ? Do you *understand* to some degree the significance and value of His costly sacrifice? Do you *grieve* your sins? Do you harbor sin, or withhold forgiveness in your heart? Do you *desire* to follow Christ more fully? If you can answer questions such as these with a clear conscience, and having repented as necessary and receiving forgiveness, now partake of the Lord's Supper and do so *in remembrance of Him*. Remember what He suffered for your sake. Remember what He has so graciously provided. And, remember all that you still have to look forward to in Him.

The Lord's Supper is something we participate in corporately as the 'body' of His redeemed followers to whom this sacrament has been given, and individually in solemn reflection and remembrance of all this means for you past, present, and future. It is a distinguishing mark of a true church, and a true disciple, to honor and participate in that which Christ Himself instituted for our good and His glory. Affliction lessens and its grip upon our lives weakens when we think upon our Lord's intense suffering, His costly sacrifice, our salvation from sin; and the eternal hope we now possess in Christ. The Lord's Supper was given to us in remembrance of these things.

Baptism

The second sacrament the Lord Jesus Christ instituted for His people is the sacrament of baptism (Matthew 28:18-20, Acts 2:38, 8:29, 34-39). This, like the Lord's Supper, is a "holy sign and seal of the covenant of grace... to represent Christ and his benefits; and to confirm our interest in him: as also, to put a visible difference between those that belong unto the church, and the rest of the world; and solemnly to engage them to the service to God in Christ, according to His Word."[39]

The Westminster Confession of Faith continues, "Baptism is a sacrament of the New Testament, ordained by Jesus Christ, not only for solemn admission of the party baptized into the visible church, but also, to be unto him a sign and seal of the covenant of grace... which sacrament is, by Christ's own appointment, to be continued *in his church* until the end of the world."[40]

Baptism is considered as an "initiatory sacrament" whereas the Lord's Supper is what is known in theology as a "confirmatory sacrament." God has consistently used signs of His covenant blessings as something for His chosen people to participate in and commemorate their separateness unto Him. The Old Testament sacraments are circumcision and Passover. In those times, God chose to ordain these as the covenantal signs for His people. For us today, Jesus Himself has instituted quite similarly, both baptism and the Lord's Supper.

Considering the obvious inter-testament unity which exists between the Old and the New Testament, it is easy to see that the Old Testament covenant sign was administered through circumcision beginning

---

[39] The Westminster Confession of Faith, 27.1

[40] The Westminster Confession of Faith, 28.1

as early as "eight days old" (Genesis 17:12-13). This was done as a sign of consecration, or separation, of what belongs to God versus what belongs to the world. In the same way, baptism is the Lord's New Testament sign and the seal of this same covenant of grace. He has instituted this for His own body of people likewise signifying that we belong to Him as a people separated for His glory and purposes. It is a sacrament reminding us of our spiritual union with Christ as well as our allegiance to His kingdom.

In defense of those of us who may have received baptism "unknowingly" as an infant and that perhaps it is invalid and does not apply; it should be noted that in the Old Testament we read that Abraham <u>and</u> his household were to be circumcised unto to God as the outward sign of God's covenant made with him (Genesis 17:7-14). Children, then, have always been special to God and are in no way limited or excluded from His assembly of people (Ezra 10:1, Luke 18:16, Psalm 127:3, Mark 9:36-37). They received that sign, that separateness of circumcision back then, just as many children have received its New Testament counterpart for us today; baptism (Acts 2:39, 3:25, 16:14-15, 30-33, c.f. Isaiah 44:3, 54:13).

Baptism then, as the outward sign of God's covenant made with his chosen assembly of people, "is not tied to that moment wherein it is administered."[41] As a covenantal sign of consecration or separation

---

[41] The Westminster Confession of Faith, 28.6

unto God, its efficacy is not limited spatially, but rather, may be administered to infants of believing parents that God's grace and His covenant promises may also include them "according to the counsel of God's will, in his appointed time."[42] Therefore, this sacrament of baptism need only once be administered unto any person.

Some may balk at this because we may have been led to believe that salvation comes through our baptism rather than, or in conjunction with, our faith. This is false. Salvation comes instantaneously in the moment of our rebirth when the grace and faith received from God elicits our confession through both our mouth and heart (Ephesians 2:5, 8, Colossians 2:13, John 3:5, Romans 10:9-10). We are saved when our election becomes manifested during the effectual inward call of the gospel of our salvation (Ephesians 1:13). It does not hang suspended in the air until we are baptized. Our faith and all included spiritual benefits are applied in the moment of belief, not sometime after it. Dr. David B. Garner has rightly said, "In the divine accomplishment of redemption, the Spirit binds us to Christ. At the moment of faith, the Spirit *applies the work of Christ immediately*, personally, and savingly."[43]

---

[42] The Westminster Confession of Faith, 28.6

[43] Dr. David B. Garner, quoted from his article titled "Redemption Applied" as seen in Ligonier Ministries Table Talk, April 2019, pg 27

Therefore, it is immaterial if baptism was administered as an infant, prior to the manifestation of salvation. As a covenant seal, baptism does not transfer salvation to an individual. This is the Spirit's work in the Sovereign application of redemption to the believer in the moment of God-initiated saving-faith. In sum, time has no bearing on this sacrament and therefore the repetition of it is neither necessary nor advised. Nevertheless, as an ordinance, it is important that we are baptized *if we never have been*. It is a joyous occasion to be celebrated by the Church, one Christ Himself has instituted for our unity and enjoyment. It is a blessing to affirm outwardly that we are His inwardly. It is sanctifying to consider ourselves separated unto Him and no longer aligned in allegiance to this world, and it is important that we consider ourselves to be dead to sin and alive to righteousness (1 Peter 2:24, Romans 6:11). But it is not *necessary* to our actual salvation. Unless we have already been baptized or are somehow otherwise prevented from being baptized (many prisons don't, for example) – we should not only want to be baptized but also we should make every effort *to be* baptized. Listen closely, if a person comes to faith on Sunday for example and the baptism isn't scheduled until the following week, but this person is involved in a fatal car crash before it is done – that believer is assured of heaven just as the thief on the cross was next to Jesus that day on Calvary. Salvation is by faith alone, grace alone, and through Christ alone. God's Sovereign work and purposes in your election, redemption, and salvation are not thwarted by someone's inability to be baptized. Nevertheless, those who *can* be baptized obviously should do so in obedience to Him and in celebration of everything it signifies.

People have tried to say that the thief on the cross was still under the Old Testament. Therefore, some contend that he made it to heaven the way he did because baptism as a New Testament ordinance had not yet gone into effect. But a closer look at Scripture reveals this to be untrue.

The writer of Hebrews refers to Jesus as "the mediator of a new covenant, so that those who are called may receive the promised eternal inheritance since a death has occurred that redeems them from the transgressions committed under the first covenant." He goes on to say, "For where a will is involved, the death of the one who made it must be established. *For a will takes effect only at death, since it is not in force as long as the one who made it is alive*" (Hebrews 9:15-17 emphasis mine).

In other words, the details and ordinances of this new covenant were made effective at the moment of Jesus' death. And so the next obvious question is who died first that day, Jesus or the thief?

The Gospel of John gives us our answer. Chapter 19:31-34 provides the necessary details. To summarize, crucified bodies were not to remain on the cross on the Sabbath. To speed up the process of dying the Roman soldiers routinely broke the legs of those who were still alive. Historically, we understand this was to speed up asphyxiation by preventing the victim from pushing themselves up in an effort to fill their lungs with air. Verse 32 mentions the soldiers breaking the legs of both thieves who had been crucified with Jesus. "But when they came to Jesus and saw that he was *already dead*, they did not break his legs" (John 19:33 emphasis mine).

The obvious conclusion is that *the new covenant began and was already in full effect before the thief died.* His crucifixion prevented him from being baptized but in no way disrupted his eternal salvation or entrance into his heavenly destination.

Thus, unless you already have been baptized a new believer should wholeheartedly desire baptism for all the reasons previously stated above. But, if death comes before the fulfillment of this Christ-given ordinance, Scripture clearly reveals that heaven will most certainly be your home.

Now, as our baptized children come to faith in the Lord Jesus, and those of us who are of age as well, we teach that we are "united in Christ so as to be partakers of all his blessings."[44] It is through our union with Christ in His death, burial, and resurrection that we are made alive, redeemed, justified, sanctified, and glorified. "We are washed from our sins by the blood of Christ"[45] through the working and the washing of the Holy Spirit of God (Titus 3:5, John 3: 5). For those who were not baptized as an infant but instead

---

[44] Calvin, Institutes 4.15. Section 6 heading, pg 858

[45] Calvin, Institutes 4.15.4, pg 860

enter into the church community as a new convert previously "outside the covenant context of the church, baptism is a vivid symbol of closure with their old life, as well as commencement of a new Christian life."[46]

In this way, baptism is joyfully celebrated individually and corporately, physically and spiritually. For the new believer, it is individually a moment of expression and commitment in purpose. Baptism is also celebrated corporately by the congregation family as a reminder of our commitment and allegiance to Jesus Christ and faithful obedient Christian living. It, therefore, affects everyone in some way. It is a call to everyone present that we are to obey God, turn from sin, strive for holiness, and live as God's consecrated people in this fallen world. Having been cleansed by the blood of Christ and the power of the Holy Spirit, we now "fore sake the world, crucify our old nature, and walk in a new and holy life."[47] Collectively, baptism teaches the new believer and the seasoned saints the *accountability* that comes with our commitment to Christ.

Do you see the individual and corporate value of the Lord's sacraments? How they combine the benefit of an individual as well as the covenant body of Christ as a whole? These sacraments then, administered within the church, are part of God's design and function for His covenant people – for our good, and to His glory.

---

[46] The Heidelberg Catechism, lord's Day 26, 269-71, pg 771

[47] The Heidelberg Catechism, lord's Day 26, 269-71, pg 771

Have you given your heart and your life to Christ? Are you faithful to this allegiance you once professed? Confess and repent of what shortcomings may exist. Make things right between you and God who's Word promises us; "if we confess our sins, he is faithful and just to forgive us our sins *and to cleanse us from all unrighteousness*" (John 1: 9). This fountain of forgiveness forever flows "without money and without price" (Isaiah 55:1). When the filth of sin muddies the water of our lives, the blood of Jesus cleanses, purifies, and makes us whole again.

As God's covenant people, baptism is an appointed sign that we are His and that our lives belong to Him. It is a distinguishing mark of a true church to rightly administer this Christ-given sacrament, teaching and celebrating the beautiful and gracious significance of it.

Christian Discipline Within the Body

The third and final distinguishing mark of a "true church" is the proper exercise of discipline within the body of Christ. The simple mention of the word 'proper' suggests this responsibility has the potential of being misused, but we could rightly conclude this to be the case with any endeavor on earth that places human beings in the position of making a decision. As with anything else, there should be a standard of rule to govern our actions while maintaining fairness and balance in how things are administered within the Church. Moreover, there should be much prayer, thought, and attention given to this area of responsibility that we might not err in judgment or respond either too rashly or too softly in any given situation. John Calvin notes the potential for the pendulum to swing in either extreme and he wisely concludes that church discipline is "to be done with moderation"[48] with severity being exercised sparingly in rare and limited cases. Instead, teaching offenders rather than commanding, and admonishing them toward repentance, reconciliation, and finally restoration. As loving care and attention are given to our physical bodies when unhealthy or in need of repair, likewise is Christian discipline to be properly exercised within the spiritual body of Christ, His beloved Church, for the sake of remedying the malady. This is done as needed and to the glory of our Lord in accordance with that which He desires for His covenant body of people. Therefore, the necessity of discipline combined with the sensitivity of it, demands that those involved with its administration be mature, grounded, and graceful Christians with a sense of wisdom, discernment, and God-fearing leadership. This is all to be founded on the Word of God, with love for His people and care for His body, looking to Jesus as the Head and the ultimate authority in each and every instance. As abiding shepherds, care is given to His flock in the manner we might expect Him to do so. Leadership will be

---

[48] Calvin, Institutes 4.12.12, pg 819

prayerfully chosen (1 Timothy 3:1-13, Titus 1:6-9, 2:1-8), false teaching will be addressed and remedied, or removed (Galatians 1:8-9, 2:11-14; 1 Timothy 6:3-10, Hebrews 13:9, 1 Corinthians 11:3). Some transgressions will require gentle correction (Galatians 6:1, Romans 15:1-2, 1 Corinthians 4:21), yet others will need firm rebuke (Ephesians 5:11-12, 1 Timothy 5:20, Titus 1:13, 2:15); and in some cases removal from the body until repentance, reconciliation, restoration can be achieved (1 Corinthians 5:1-5, 9-13; c.f. 2 Corinthians 2:5-11). If restoration isn't possible, then ex-communication is a last resort.

Some may ask, why is discipline necessary if we are all "believers" having been equally justified by the blood of Christ; why then this distinction in governing appropriate doctrine and behavior? Simply put, Church discipline is vital to its health, growth, general maintenance, and overall well-being. In fact, what other known entity could function successfully without wisdom, discernment, and correction? Moreover, as we have already discussed, the Church exists as a mixed body of sheep and goats, wheat and tares, lost and saved (Matthew 13:24-30, 22:11-14, 25:31-32, Luke 13:24-27). Therefore, oversight is necessary to maintain the direction of the Church in a forward and upward direction. In fact, churches that neglect the responsibility of Christian discipline are most prone to fatal doctrinal error, rampant sin within the congregation, divine displeasure, and a damaged and ineffective witness to the world we live in. Appropriate discipline within the body of

Christ is therefore a distinguishing mark of a true church and should be considered as important and necessary as the pure preaching of God's Word and the administration of his sacraments, the Lord's Supper, and Baptism.

The issue we face with this third distinguishing mark, unfortunately, and perhaps you the reader have experienced, is the reality that sometimes our feelings may get hurt if we find ourselves on the receiving end of a rebuke or consultation. I cannot stress enough that the proper exercise of church discipline must include genuine love and concern for the brother or sister in question. Everything about the approach, manner of speaking, and our conversation must stem from Christ-like concern for their well-being. The aim in mind is to help the person see and overcome any sinful attitude or behavior that needs correction in a manner and depth consistent with the offense. Nevertheless, I am aware that even in such cases where all this has been done lovingly and consistent with Scripture, people still recoil at the attempt and then harbor bitterness against what they perceive to be an intrusion into 'their business.' With so many other places of worship to choose from sometimes the decision is made to relocate to a different church down the road, or worse, quit altogether. But in doing so, we miss the point of discipline while also robbing ourselves of its intended purpose-designed for our good.

People that don't typically overreact when a physician points out a habit we need to change or discontinue since it is damaging to our health or get mad if surgery is needed to remove cancerous cells; why then are we so reluctant or hypersensitive in receiving correction in the spiritual sense? As believers, we are sometimes too prone to becoming blind to our sin. To safeguard against it, simple accountability keeps us from continuing too far in the wrong direction. God might use a brother or sister in Christ to help us see our need to turn things around. Owning up to it and then doing something about it is a mark of someone who loves Christ and wishes to grow and mature in Him as His disciple. Contrary to this; pride, bitterness, and stubbornness will stagnate any progress spiritually, while also greatly dishonoring the Lord and grieving His Holy Spirit within us. Why do this? Is it possible that what the Bible and the church have said regarding our sin is true? Why not humbly accept the correction and change our course? What prevents you from reconciling with God, and one another?

Think of King David and how he had done so good for so long, yet ended up living in gross sin, like committing adultery with Bathsheba. Having stolen another man's wife, sleeping with her, killing her husband, and descending into further disobedience and irresponsibility as a servant of God; David in a sense became blind to his own sin (2 Samuel 11:1-26). The first verse in 2nd Samuel Chapter 12 begins with, "And the Lord sent Nathan to David." We know this was done to expose David's sin and his obvious blindness and disregard to it. As a result, the Holy Spirit convicted David of his sin (2 Samuel 12:13) and led him to repentance from his transgressions (Psalm 51:1-17), which thereby restored his relationship with God. We should welcome the Nathans in our lives and examine closely whether the things they are saying hold true. Like David, maybe we've become blind or calloused to our actions and the Lord has sent His servant to shine the light in this dark corner of our life, founded in love, genuine concern, and for the sake of repentance, reconciliation, and restoration. That is the purpose of this third distinguishing mark of a true Church, and where we worship should rightly administer this important aspect concerning the body of Christ. We should therefore not only seek a place of worship that rightly exercises church discipline within the body of Christ, but we should also seek to understand its design, function and respond graciously and obediently if ever subjected to it.

Are you holding onto bitterness or rebellion against the Church or one of its servants? By God's grace and mercy can you find it in your heart to forgive the person if necessary; and with the Holy Spirits' help can you let go of whatever sin that comes between you and God – or faithfully attending church?

We should be very cautious in shunning the corporate assembly of believers, for in doing so we are increasingly susceptible to doubt, depression, discouragement, and despondency. Furthermore, to walk away altogether, never to return is a sure sign that we didn't truly belong to Him in the first place. To fall away completely and finally reveals that our temporary religion was just a work of the flesh void of actual Holy Spirit regeneration (1 John 2:19, 1 Corinthians 11:18-19, 2 Peter 2:21-22). Are you willingly resisting corporate worship with other believers? Do you forsake the opportunity to partake in the sacraments Christ instituted for the good of His Church? Are you not gathered together to hear the Word of God in community with the rest of His sheep? If this is the result of pride, bitterness, or holding onto a past offense or grudge; I pray you will take it to the Lord for the grace and wisdom to make things right. Often, when we forgive someone who has wronged us in the past, it unlocks a sense of spiritual freedom as it liberates us from the unnecessary weight we've held onto for so long. Forgiveness has a way of dissolving the angst we feel while in affliction, and it speeds up the process of restoring our spiritual vigor. For this reason, we should honestly examine ourselves, whether there is any blockage restricting the flow of God's love and grace in, or out, of our hearts. If your absence from church is a result of stubbornness, conflict, or past hurt, choose to resolve this today in honor and obedience to Jesus who unites redeemed sinners through His sacrificial death, burial, and glorious resurrection. As the Cornerstone and the Head of His Church, and through this eternal union we now share with Him, Christ calls us as ambassadors to His Kingdom, to live as children of the light in one accord with one another, looking to Him as the Author and Finisher of our faith. We prove to be His children when we imitate Him, model His behavior, obey what He has commanded, utilize what He has graciously provided, and when we walk as He did in love, forgiveness, sacrifice, and perseverance. Pause now and ask yourself, what prevents you from doing so? He is a faithful teacher, example, forgiver, and obstacle remover. He beckons His children to beseech His help in walking rightly before Him. God's covenant people are forever encouraged to seek their covenant maker. I pray you will do so today.

CHAPTER 6 - BETTER TOGETHER

MAY NOTHING EVER DISCOURAGE OR dissuade you from participating in the corporate worship, praise, assembly, sanctification, and unity of God's chosen people. We need each other. Every part of His "body" matters. None of us were designed to live this Christian life, nor wrestle the affliction and trials we experience, in isolation from other believers or absent from the means of grace God has provided for His Church. If you have been away, for any length of time and any multitude of reasons, please come back.

Years ago while I was being discipled by a dear friend and fellow soldier of the Lord, Weston Benoy, he shared a helpful illustration about the importance of fellowship within the body of Christ which still rings true today. The story he gave was of a man who at one time had been faithfully attending his church until a 'storm' entered his life and he decided to deal with things on his own. In his despondency, he faded away from worship and fellowship spending most of his time in front of the fireplace depressed about the affliction he now found himself burdened with. His pastor took notice that the man had not been coming to services so he drove over to his house and knocked on the door. After a few minutes, the man opened the door and then went back to his chair without saying a word. His pastor then followed the man to his living room and sat quietly in the chair that was beside him. Both the men gazed at the fire in silence for some time. The pastor thought for a moment, stood up, and went over to the fireplace. He took the long-handled tongs and without saying anything, reached in and removed one of the hot coals, setting it on the brick. He sat back down again. Both he and the man watched as this burning coal flickered red, changed to orange, and then slowly faded until it eventually went out, extinguished. After a moment the pastor stood up. Using the tongs, he took the black coal and placed it with the others still in the fire. The coal re-ignited again and resumed its bright red glow. The man looked up with a grin and said, "Thanks for the fiery sermon." The pastor placed his hand on the man's shoulder, smiled, and said, "See you Sunday."

We belong together, never in isolation from one another. We are knitted and joined together by the Holy Spirit of God. It is His design that we grow and mature in our faith together, with unity as our goal. We are God's workmanship, His covenant people who make up His "body," the Church, which we belong to individually, corporately, physically, and spiritually. We are vitally connected to Jesus as a branch is to the vine. We receive our faith sustaining nourishment through Him, His Word, His sacraments, even as we bring Him our corporate worship and praise.

As His redeemed children we will one day stand before His throne to worship and serve Him forever.

Before going to the cross, Jesus told His disciples, "I will build My Church…." (Matthew 16:18). He also promised them, "I will come again" (John 14:3). If the Master were to return within this lifetime, what would He find us doing? How would He find us acting? It is not too late to change our course and make things right again. Just as repentance from sin accompanied saving faith in God's work of salvation, it is likewise an integral part of our lifelong journey with Christ. Many of us have experienced times throughout this "walk" when the flesh has won over the Spirit and we have given in to worldly thoughts and practices. These influences work as a current that attempts to pull us away from our foundation in Christ. Such behaviors and thought patterns are introduced by the devil who still tries to convince people today, thousands of years after the Fall, that we can do things on our own, with human wisdom, and in our own strength. Just as he lied to Adam and Eve so long ago in the Garden of Eden, he continues to lie and tempt God's people today. Within the body of Christ, the devil wants division. He promotes self-centeredness. He entices us toward pride, envy, and judgment of others. Where has he most tempted you?

The Apostle John writes, "Little children, you are from God and have overcome them, for he who is in you is greater than he who is in the world" (John 4:4). As God's covenant people, we already possess all the divine power and presence necessary to walk in victory. We are no longer in bondage to sin; we are free (John 8: 36). Anyone who is in Christ has died to sin. Our old self was crucified with Him in order that the body of sin might be brought to nothing so that we would no longer be enslaved to sin (Romans 6:6). Those chains have been broken and removed by Christ Jesus. Sin, therefore, no longer has any dominion over you (Romans 6:9).

We sometimes lose sight of this fact. In the weakness of our flesh and in yielding to temptation we may allow the self to dictate our decisions and guide the path of our lives. But doing so never leads us close to Jesus or honors Him in any way. If you have veered off the path and have ended up in a spiritual pit, He extends His capable hand today to place your feet on solid ground (Psalm 37: 23-24, 28:9, 40:2).

Have you allowed pride, selfishness, bitterness, jealousy, or resentment to drive a wedge between you and the corporate Christian assembly in fellowship and worship? Confess it to Him today. Renew your vows and your commitment. Remember your accountability. Just as God has promised never to leave or forsake us, it is wise spiritual practice for us to make this same promise *to Him.*

Do feelings of unworthiness keep you bound in isolation? None of us are worthy to stand in God's presence! Only in Christ and because of Christ are we made worthy. As His church we glory in the righteousness He has imputed to us. We lift our voices, hearts, and our lives to thank our King of

Glory for taking our sin and its debt on the cross and dying for our iniquities. Jesus died for us while we were yet sinners. Before Christ, we were filthy, fallen, corrupt, and ungodly. Yet He willingly stretched wide His arms, nailed to that cross, that He would lovingly embrace sinners just like you and me. He took us as we are. It is Christ alone who justifies, sanctifies – He *makes us* new creatures now worthy to stand in God's glorious presence forever.

Charles Spurgeon once told a story of a man who planned to paint a picture of a city landscape. Within the scope of his desired painting lay a homeless man wearing filthy rags that were in tatters. Wanting to capture the fullest realism of this scene, he went over to the man and politely invited him to his art studio so that would be part of this anticipated painting. The next day before his appointed visit, this homeless man had received a haircut, bathed, shaved, found a change of clothes, and in every sense had made every effort to clean himself up. Having done so, he went over to the painter's art studio as promised, and he knocked on the door. As the painter opened it he was taken back in surprise, hardly recognizing the man. "What have you done?" He asked. "I needed you as you are," he said. *Come as you are.*

In the priceless painting of eternal redemption of sinners, God had graciously chosen to include homeless vagabonds just like us. He took our filthy rags and all of our sinful unworthiness and He is changing us inwardly "to be conformed to the image of His Son" (Romans 8:29). *He* justifies and sanctifies us before the Father having robed us in His own obedience and righteousness. God called us in all our filth, inability, and unworthiness to come as we are.

God's work is most greatly displayed in broken vessels that are plain, empty, and fully surrendered to Him. From fallen and sinful humanity, God has drawn out His body of people, the Church; and has delivered us out of the domain of darkness and He has thereby transferred us to the kingdom of His beloved Son, in whom we have redemption through His blood, the forgiveness of sins (Colossians 1:13-14).

As our loving Father, He now calls us to "walk in a manner worthy of the calling to which you have been called, with all humility and gentleness, with patience, bearing with one another in love, eager to maintain the unity of the Spirit in the bond of peace. There is one body and one Spirit – just as you were called to the one hope that belongs to your call – one Lord, one faith, one baptism, one God and father of all, who is over all and through all and in all" (Ephesians 4:1-6).

It is His desire that we would be forever connected to Him, focused on Him, and living sacrifices for Him and to His glory. Our Sovereign God and Creator has graciously cleansed our souls and has gifted us with everlasting life that we may live and reign with Him as we praise his Holy name together with the angels and the heavenly hosts. We are a prepared people heading for a prepared place.

Through our union with Him, and consequently with each other; we are better together. We are stronger together. And we function according to God's will and His design for His church when we operate in unity utilizing the gifts He has given us for "building up the body of Christ, until we all attain to the unity of the faith and of the knowledge of the Son of God, to mature manhood, to the measure of the stature of the fullness of Christ, so that we may no longer be children, tossed to and fro by the waves and carried about by every wind of doctrine, by human cunning, by craftiness in deceitful schemes. Rather, speaking the truth in love we are to grow up in every way into him who is the head, into Christ, from whom the whole body, joined and held together by every joint which is equipped when each part is working properly, makes the body grow so that it builds itself up in love" (Ephesians 4:12-16). Let us be trustworthy and faithful stewards of all He has entrusted to us and in obedience to that which He has commanded us.

In closing, let us turn our attention to Paul's timeless prayer to the Ephesians. First that they might come to know and comprehend God's love for them. Then, with that as the foundation, that they would come to love one another in Christ Unity.

He writes, "that according to the riches of His glory He may grant you to be strengthened with power through His Spirit in your inner being, so that Christ may dwell in your hearts through faith – that you, being rooted and grounded in love, may have the strength to comprehend with all the saints what is the breadth and length and height and depth, and to know the love of Christ that surpasses knowledge, that you may be filled with all the fullness of God.

Now to Him who is able to do far more abundantly than all that we ask or think, according to the power at work within us, to Him be glory *in the church* and Christ Jesus throughout all generations, forever and ever. Amen" (Ephesians 3:16-20).

May any obstacle preventing our adherence to faithful obedience be resolved and removed as we deny the world, the flesh, or the devil to hinder us any longer. Ignite the flame of godly desire and renew the warm glow of worship and fellowship. The body of Christ isn't the same without you.